Abuse and Survival:

A Fact File

MEMBERS OF
'SURVIVING DAMAGE IN CHILDHOOD'
ADVISORY GROUP

Dr John Coleman,
Director, Trust for the
Study of Adolescence

Prof. Peter Wedge,
School of Health and Social Work,
University of East Anglia

Peter Wilson,
Director, Young Minds

Dr Susan Bailey,
Consultant Adolescent
Forensic Psychiatrist,
Mental Health Services of Salford

Brian Waller,
Director, Leicestershire
Social Services Department

Roger Graef,
Writer and Broadcaster

Dr Fiona Caldicott,
The Principal, Somerville College,
Oxford University

Prof. Peter Hill,
Academic Dept. of Psychiatry,
St. George's Hospital Medical School

John Harding,
Chief Probation Officer,
Inner London Probation Service

Prof. David Berridge,
Dept. of Professional Social Studies,
University of Luton

Dr Ruth Sinclair,
Director of Research,
National Children's Bureau

Dr Gwyneth Boswell,
Senior Lecturer, School of Social Work,
University of East Anglia

Compiled and written
by Dr Nicola Madge
National Children's Bureau

Assisted by Steve Howell

Produced by
The Prince's Trust – Action

In association with
The National Children's Bureau

NATIONAL
CHILDREN'S
BUREAU
The powerful voice
for the child

Published by The Prince's Trust – Action

© The Prince's Trust – Action

First published 1997

British Library Cataloguing in Publication Data

A catalogue record of this book is available from the British Library

ISBN 1 902243 00 5

Photography – Luke Golobitsh
Printed by T.J. International, Padstow, Cornwall

Designed and produced in Great Britain
by Wild Associates, 2a Ewell Road, Cheam, Surrey SM3 8BU

contents

'Because I trust you about as much as I trust
my cat with a bird, and that is to say about as much
as I trust anyone who isn't me...'

'And you should understand that I can't tell you
how to make it better or
how to teach me to trust you or
how to get near me when I push you away.'

'I can only tell you
what little I know
and that is all that you see
and that is, how I survived.'

(Malone and others, 1996)

setting the scene

Thousands of children and young people in Britain today suffer the immediate trauma of physical or sexual abuse. Many survive and cope well, but others are less fortunate and left with lasting scars.

This Fact File looks at the nature, extent and effects of childhood abuse and tries to identify factors linked with survival. How do many young people manage, despite all the odds, to grow up as normally functioning, successful and well-adjusted adults? Are they more resilient? Are they helped by formal and informal support?

Abuse is sometimes blamed for juvenile crime, drug and alcohol misuse, prostitution and a range of other social problems which not only cause distress to young people and others but are also very expensive to deal with. And it is held responsible for less visible effects on self-esteem, depression and general emotional well-being. Preventing abuse and lessening its impact can therefore have far-reaching benefits.

A range of relevant interventions is examined in the Fact File and is supplemented by lists of useful contacts, addresses and reference materials at the end.

It is worth noting at the outset that physical and sexual abuse, the main focus of the Fact File, have much in common with other adversities encountered in many young lives. Children severely bullied by other pupils at school, or harassed and discriminated against because of their racial background are, for example, also very real victims of abuse. Their distress and difficulties, as well as the ways in which they may be helped to cope and become more resilient, can be very similar.

> *'One day maybe I will have the answers. Until then I will put up with hurt. I've coped with it for forty-plus years and I have no doubt I'll cope with it for a few more. Maybe if there had been helplines I could have turned to I would have coped better – I don't know. What I do know is that the memories never go away, they are always there lurking in the background.'*
>
> *(Gordon, 1994)*

SOME KEY FACTS

- some three per thousand children and teenagers under 18 years are, at any time, named on child protection registers in England;

- almost twice this number are registered at some point during the course of a year;

- around 40 per cent of these children are considered at risk of physical injury and some 22 per cent are at risk of sexual abuse;

- a further unknown, and probably large, number of young people experience abuse which does not come to the attention of child protection agencies;

- more than 2,300 people were convicted in English courts during 1994 for sexual offences involving children under 16 years, and a further 1,700 admitted guilt and were cautioned;

- concern about continuing abuse in children's residential homes has led to a series of national and local inquiries in the last decade;

- over 15,000 children and young people a year telephone ChildLine to talk about sexual or physical abuse and some 800 adults seek help for their own past or continuing childhood abuse;

- research studies suggest that between one third and a half of abused children develop psychiatric disorders or other problems in the short- or longer-term;

- *However*, up to two-thirds of abused young people have no enduring difficulties; and

- despite some initiatives, there remains a real shortage of help and support for adult survivors of childhood abuse.

'it is clear that the number of children involved in harmful or potentially harmful situations is large and that there are no obvious signs of those numbers diminishing.'

(National Commission of Inquiry into the Prevention of Child Abuse, 1996)

patterns of abuse **2**

DEFINING ABUSE

Many different definitions of physical and sexual abuse are adopted by clinicians, research studies, agencies and services – and indeed by survivors themselves. For the purposes of this Fact File, abuse means genuine acts of cruelty rather than bad parenting or circumstances which are indirectly harmful to children.

Physical abuse is particularly difficult to define, and there is a sizeable grey area between the smacking and physical punishment that most children experience at some time and significant physical injury. There is, however, little disagreement that particularly severe actions resulting in harm are abusive.

The term **sexual abuse** has been used to describe a range of experiences from witnessing a single instance of self-exposure at one extreme to repeated and coercive sexual intercourse at the other. At the more serious end, child sexual abuse might be defined as:

> *'The involvement of dependent children and adolescents in sexual activities with an adult, or any person older or bigger, in which the child is used as a sexual object for the gratification of the older person's needs or desires, and to which the child is unable to give consent due to the unequal power in the relationship.'*
>
> (Sanderson, 1990)

Over the past decade or so the description and classification of physical and sexual abuse have become more complicated as further contexts and characteristics have been identified.

Organised abuse is the term now often applied to abuse – usually sexual but also physical – which is, as its name implies, in some sense planned. Definitions vary but more than one perpetrator is generally involved (some descriptions include multiple perpetrators and may state that at least one of these must not live in the family home), who may or may not previously be known to the victims. Characteristically it is the premeditated and systematic abuse, often over a considerable period of time, of a young person or persons who are specially targeted, 'groomed' and abused.

When organised abuse occurs in institutions, such as children's homes, schools or day-care centres, it is sometimes referred to as **institutional abuse**. In these settings the

> *'Morris had [total] hold over our lives at the school, at home, the lot. He had us right where he wanted us, under his thumb. He was a very convincing man.'*
>
> (Bibby, 1996)

abuser(s) may use plausibility or authority to recruit children for sexual abuse and for some young people, may come to dominate their lives.

More controversially, organised abuse may also include (although various terms are used) **ritual abuse** which implies sexual abuse with allegations of ritual or ceremony, and **satanic abuse** in which ritual abuse is said to include the worship of Satan.

Finally, organised abuse may refer to networks of abusers in **paedophile** and **sex rings**. A high level of co-operation can exist within these networks which use multiple victims and may trade in pornography and/or prostitution for commercial profit.

The criteria for intervention

Statutory agencies need to know when they are required to intervene and take action, and the Children Act 1989 accordingly introduced the idea of 'thresholds' which initiate and determine the child protection process. It also notes that the crucial criterion for intervention in cases of child abuse is one of 'significant harm' where:

- 'harm' means ill-treatment or impairment of health or development;

- 'development' means physical, intellectual, emotional, social or behavioural development;

- 'health' means physical or mental health;

- 'ill-treatment' includes sexual abuse and forms of ill-treatment which are not physical; and

- where 'whether harm suffered by a child is significant turns on the child's health or development, his health or development shall be compared with that which could reasonably be expected of a similar child.'

This definition is critical in setting the threshold for intervention and putting the responsibility to act upon statutory agencies.

THE NUMBERS INVOLVED

Just as definitions of abuse vary so do estimates of the young people affected. Numbers are hard to assess as abuse is, by its very nature, a 'secretive' crime. People who abuse others do not usually own up, and the abused frequently do not tell. Child protection registers held by social services departments or agencies such as the NSPCC, or police records, document the proportion of cases that come to light – but are much more likely to include families from more disadvantaged than better-off homes. Registers also do not always distinguish between children known to have been abused and those who seem to be 'at risk'.

Asking adults to recall childhood abuse does not lead to any more reliable figures. Studies have suggested rates of sexual abuse ranging from as low as three per cent of the population to as high as over 60 per cent. Not only is the meaning of an experience somewhat subjective, but it is widely recognised that people can forget things that have happened in the past just as they may 'remember' things that have not. Survivors who speak out through surveys, helplines or autobiography are a special group and, whether selected for study due to a clinical condition or other circumstance, or self-motivated to tell their own story, are unlikely to be typical.

In practice, evidence on abused young people comes mainly from social agency records, callers to telephone helplines, clinical reports, research studies, biography or autobiography. Some additional details are available from official statistics and enquiries. These sources give an indication of the scale of the problem:

- the NSPCC estimates from national homicide figures that one or two children die each week as the result of abuse or neglect;

- 32,351 children, or 29 per 10,000 population aged under 18 years, were named on child protection registers in England at the end of March 1996;

- approximately four in ten of these children were considered at risk of physical abuse and almost a quarter at risk of sexual abuse;

- organised abuse is rarely mentioned on child protection registers and there is insufficient available information to be able to say how often it occurs;

- some 160,000 young people are drawn into the child protection process each year although the majority of these are not registered; and

- a London study of over one thousand 16–21 year-olds found that four per cent of the women and two per cent of the men reported severe sexual abuse.

These figures almost certainly underestimate the true extent of severe physical and sexual abuse.

WHO IS AT PARTICULAR RISK OF ABUSE?

Certain young people are at greater risk of abuse than others and it would seem, from the available information, that the following factors are influential:

- **sex:** while boys and girls are almost equally likely to be named on child protection registers for physical injury, boys are more frequently known to have been physically abused; girls are almost twice as likely to be on registers for sexual abuse and are also far more often reported as abused; outside the home, boys seem at more risk and males abusing boys is an important feature distinguishing organised abuse from sexual abuse within the family; both boys and girls are, however, targeted by paedophiles;

- **age:** the incidence of reported physical abuse tends to decrease with age (although recent American data suggests it may resurge among teenagers) while the likelihood of sexual abuse increases; there are, however, sex differences in these patterns;

- **disability:** children (and older people) with disabilities are at above average risk for all forms of abuse; some studies have pointed to the particular difficulties they present for their parents, and others to their vulnerability;

- **family type:** children on risk child protection registers are more likely than others from similar social groups not to be living with both their natural parents; however, this is partly because families experiencing disadvantage and breakdown are more likely to come to notice;

- **vulnerability:** it is suggested that the victims of organised abuse are frequently vulnerable, insecure and easy to manipulate. For these reasons they might include those from unhappy home backgrounds as well as those with learning difficulties where the risk of 'telling' might be less;

- **personality and behaviour:** it has been reported that aggressive young males may be targeted for abuse and recruitment to networks of perpetrators operating in institutions such as children's homes;

- **ethnicity:** there are conflicting views and reports on the links between abuse and ethnic background and this is an area in which no firm conclusions can be drawn; and

- **social disadvantage:** agency records indicate that the majority of families in which abuse is detected are on low incomes, unemployed, and in semi-skilled or unskilled work. Self-report studies, however, suggest that serious abuse can occur in any type of family background.

WHO ARE THE ABUSERS?

From what is known it appears that:

- most sexual abuse is carried out by adult males known to the young people involved, and natural fathers or father substitutes (who may or may not be living with them at the time) are involved in about half of all instances;

- fathers or father substitutes are also involved in around half of all cases of physical injury;

- mothers are rarely reported as involved in sexual abuse although they are implicated in about a third of instances of physical injury;

- nonetheless, around one per cent of girls and 16 per cent of boys calling ChildLine describe sexual assaults by their mothers;

- the perpetrator is an adolescent or younger teenager, perhaps an older brother, in up to one third of cases of sexual abuse, although rarely in instances of physical injury;

- other relatives, friends of the family, and neighbours, are also sometimes implicated in sexual abuse;

- paedophiles include both homosexual and heterosexual men;

- the main factors precipitating abuse in families known to social agencies are overwhelming stress and social problems; in a small proportion a parent may have a serious psychiatric problem or there may be a context of marital violence; and

- sexual offenders can abuse large numbers of young people; one American study estimated that the average adolescent sexual offender might go on to commit 380 sex crimes over his lifetime.

'We still have a problem getting people to believe that, yes a nice man like that, who all his colleagues and friends and neighbours think is marvellous, can abuse children. People who are accused almost always deny it...'

(Rickford, 1993)

Most abuse occurs in ordinary families and by ordinary people. Indeed, those who abuse can be hard to recognise.

links with later problems **3**

Numerous personal accounts, research studies, clinical reports and reviews have linked abuse with later problems in adolescence and early adulthood, and this section outlines some of the main negative outcomes described whether physical or sexual abuse is implicated. Causal links are rarely possible to prove, and contradictory conclusions may sometimes arise from research and personal testimony. The fact that a multitude of interrelated difficulties can arise in the later lives of abused children is, however, the important point.

'Abuse is like throwing a stone into a lake, the ripples are endless.'

(Stanley, 1994)

EFFECTS IN THE SHORT-TERM

Mistreatment of any kind is likely to cause initial misery – whether or not the effects last or lead to later problems. Among reported outcomes of sexual abuse are fear, poor concentration, temper tantrums, anger and hostility, guilt and shame, lowered self-esteem, depression, inappropriate sexual behaviour, bed-wetting and sleep disturbances.

It is impossible to say how often these short-term reactions occur, and whether they are directly attributable to the abuse, as studies present inconsistent findings. There is some agreement, however, that between one and two in every five children seen by clinicians show pathological disturbance in the immediate aftermath of sexual abuse.

Recently there has been considerable interest in the concept of post-traumatic stress disorder in which trauma is persistently re-experienced through, for example, dreams, flashbacks or intrusive thoughts for, by definition, a period of at least one month. How useful this is for describing damage from abuse is, however, debatable.

'Child abuse has been described by some as the "critical link" to most problems of youth and later adulthood... Experts in the field cite an indisputable relationship between child abuse and a range of disorders. In some studies, 90 per cent of individuals exhibiting serious difficulties experienced abusive childhoods.'

(Katz, 1997)

DIFFICULTIES AT SCHOOL

Other early emotional reactions to abuse may be academic and behaviour problems at school. Most studies of parents or teachers suggest that abused schoolchildren are particularly likely to underachieve and behave badly, and to bully or be bullied. These conclusions must, however, be viewed with caution. First, the pupils are not usually compared with clinical samples and it may be that their problems reflect other difficulties in their daily lives rather than the experience of abuse itself. And second, self-ratings by children are not so clear-cut and indicate less striking differences between abused and non-abused groups.

ANTI-SOCIAL BEHAVIOUR

In some cases a history of abuse is linked to behaviour rather worse than just 'acting badly'. Research has shown that abused children can develop such marked social and emotional difficulties that they become extremely aggressive and particularly likely to be arrested for juvenile delinquency or criminal behaviour in later years.

One study on the early background of violent young offenders, carried out for The Prince's Trust, provides an illustration. Of 200 Section 53 offenders – children and young people who kill or commit other grave (usually violent) crimes – around three in ten had experienced sexual abuse, four in ten physical abuse, and a small proportion organised or ritual abuse. Almost a third had suffered emotional abuse. Overall, more than a quarter experienced at least two of these forms of abuse and almost three-quarters at least one. Most of the sexually abused offenders were males abused by males at home. Some had gone on to be abused again, usually in residential children's homes or through contacts with homosexual men.

EMOTIONAL DISTRESS

A Department of Health document has claimed that 'All abuse involves some emotional ill-treatment' with likely adverse effects on children's emotional and behavioural development. Certainly survivors who wrote to the National Commission of Inquiry into the Prevention of Child Abuse seemed more affected in the longer-term by emotional distress than by the physical injury or sexual abuse itself.

Emotional distress in later life can take many forms. It may be shown in low self-esteem, guilt, social isolation or emotional difficulties reflected in behaviours such as eating disorders or feeling suicidal as outlined below. In contrast to much 'acting out' behaviour, emotional problems may remain hidden.

'How can I complain when there are no marks which can be seen. The hurt is inside. I feel like I am nothing – when you say that out loud to someone it is almost like admitting you're nothing. After all if your mum and dad think you're nothing, you are nothing.'

(National Commission of Inquiry into the Prevention of Child Abuse, 1996)

DEPRESSION AND PSYCHIATRIC DISTURBANCE

Evidence suggests that both physically and sexually abused children can develop psychiatric disorders which may last throughout life, but the evidence is mixed on the form these may take, their duration, and numbers likely to be affected. Findings depend to some extent on the groups in question. Studies looking at the consequences of abuse suggest that between one third and one half of abused children show some form of (possible lifelong) psychiatric disorder, while those looking at the early histories of clinic patients seem generally agreed that between a quarter and a half of psychiatric in–patients were abused as children.

There is no typical syndrome of psychiatric disturbance following abuse. Among children, and particularly boys, aggressive and violent behaviour appears common.

In adulthood, depression is the most frequently mentioned outcome of sexual abuse within both clinical and non-clinical samples. It seems that the sexually abused are both far *more* likely than the non-abused to become depressed in adulthood and, if they do develop major depression, far *less* likely to recover. Some studies indicate that the prognosis is particularly poor for women who have been both sexually and physically abused.

FEELING SUICIDAL

Suicidal behaviour includes thinking about suicide and deliberately harming oneself as well as actions that result in death. A variety of studies, based on clinical and non-clinical samples, have linked early abuse, especially sexual abuse, with all these aspects. Personal accounts of survivors add weight to their conclusion.

To commit, or attempt to commit, suicide is a relatively rare course of action. Sexual abuse which includes physical abuse, aggression and force may, however, increase its risk.

'I think the sexual abuse I went through when I were a little lass had something to do with some breakdowns I had. I've had three breakdowns altogether, three breakdowns... the last breakdown I have had, I was 68, I nearly done... and this one, I did... I nearly done away with myself'

(Stanley, 1994)

'About the age of sixteen I would say I was slashing my wrists and inflicting wounds on myself and the caring professions in their wisdom decided I was depressed and locked me in a mental institute. I decided I couldn't live with the past and nobody was listening to me or asking what had happened to me. I decided I just wanted to end the dark tunnel of abuse and I tried to hang myself. I can remember so vividly tying the noose round my neck and just somehow pushing the box away. I can remember my eyes were fading and for one instance I didn't want to die – I pulled feverishly at the rope and let myself drop.'

(Gordon, 1994)

FOOD, DRINK AND DRUGS

Physical and sexual abuse have been reported as risk factors for a range of eating disorders, but it would appear that the link is indirect. Although bulimia nervosa is more common than expected among people with a history of incest and other forms of abuse, it occurs in only a minority of cases. Eating disorders, where present, probably reflect general psychological distress. All the same they may help to reduce tension and stress:

> *'I was hooked on laxatives and my weight went down to seven stone. The only way I live is shutting off, it is the only way I cope. I now eat away the pain and now I am fat I feel safer, but I feel so alone.'*
>
> *(National Commission of Inquiry into the Prevention of Child Abuse, 1996)*

People commonly turn to drink and drugs when under stress, and this course may be taken by those surviving abuse. There is some empirical support for heightened consumption of alcohol amongst adults who were sexually abused as children, and the same is true for drug and substance abuse. Again it seems that the link is indirect.

DIFFICULTIES IN RELATIONSHIPS

Time and again survivors of early sexual abuse refer to problems they have had in developing relationships, whether these are with friends, relatives or sexual partners, and whether with members of the same or the opposite sex. The range of explanations for these findings suggest that a fear of intimacy, a lack of trust, a false understanding about aggression and passivity in relationships, a tendency to manipulate or be manipulated, and disturbed sexual functioning, are among the causes.

For some survivors the main outcome appears to be timidity and social isolation. Suffering quietly can, apparently, become a way of life.

Others who have outwardly coped and developed adult relationships may still have been affected.

> *'I felt very much imprisoned for many years. I was certainly emotionally disturbed and had no real friends. I don't remember playing happy games with children my own age. I seemed to spend an awful lot of time sitting in the dark in a big, tatty leather arm chair, rocking to and fro and crying silently.'*
>
> *(Gordon, 1994)*

It is much easier to chart individual histories than to describe what happens to people in general, and there is little doubt that the impact of abuse is very variable. It seems, to give an example, that early sexual abuse may be linked with either promiscuity or frigidity.
It may well be that non-abusing aspects of family life and relationships have the greatest impact on adult social, psychological and sexual functioning in abusive and non-abusive families alike.

'I hadn't experienced feelings in any true sense. I had no feelings to express, only superficial feelings, so that I really didn't know what feelings were. It certainly affected my marriage – my sense of connection with my husband was very limited. I found it affected my relationship with my children.'

(Gordon, 1994)

ONCE A VICTIM, ALWAYS A VICTIM?

There is more than anecdotal evidence that a person who has been abused once is at particular risk of further abuse – whether by people they do or do not know. Although it is difficult to be sure how often these patterns occur, studies in England and America have suggested that:

- girls who have been seriously sexually abused are at heightened risk of later rape;

- women raped on more than one occasion are particularly likely to have been abused in childhood;

- sexually abused females are much more likely than others to live with partners who physically or sexually assault them; and

- populations of juvenile prostitutes contain an overrepresentation of young women who experienced childhood sexual abuse.

There are several possible explanations for these findings. First, young people who run away from abusive backgrounds are likely to end up in 'dangerous' environments where they may be lured into prostitution or exploited in other ways. Second, their experiences may mark them out as visible targets for violent and abusive men to whom they succumb: they may in some sense be people who attract, or have learned to attract, violence. Third, they may have low self-esteem and expect little from relationships. As suggested earlier, the abused child may learn the role of the victim – and then re-enact it in adulthood.

DEPRIVATION AND DISADVANTAGE

Abuse frequently occurs in families already facing considerable deprivation and disadvantage, and it can be very difficult to say 'what has caused what' as later problems develop.

First, there is little doubt that social and environmental stress can increase the risk of abuse.

Second, abuse may directly lead to increased hardship. Thus incest could result in family breakdown and increased poverty, or perhaps to a child being taken 'into care'. Abuse may also encourage a young person to run away from home but into new problems and difficulties – including prostitution or unsuitable relationships. The complex patterns of interrelated misfortunes that can arise make it all but impossible to establish the causal links.

'Families overwhelmed and depressed by social problems form the greatest proportion of those assessed and supported by child protection agencies.'

(Department of Health, 1995)

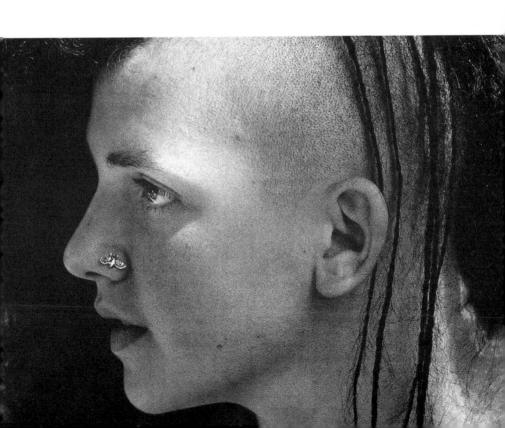

JUST MISSING OUT...

Finally, an important outcome of early abuse for some people may just be the feeling that they missed out on an ordinary childhood and family life.

> '...That's the thing that I hate the
> most – it's that I feel he took my
> life from me and he acts as if our
> childhood was normal.'
>
> (National Commission of Inquiry into the
> Prevention of Child Abuse, 1996)

The sense of loss may be triggered time and again by everyday events.

> 'Sitting in the park, I saw a girl with her dad,
> She was laughing and playing,
> The kind of trust and affection that I'd never had.
> She's had it better, I thought with an ache,
> She's had a childhood. Her dolls, her toys,
> She trusts her dad and that's no mistake,
> All the things I never could...'
>
> (Rouf, 1991)

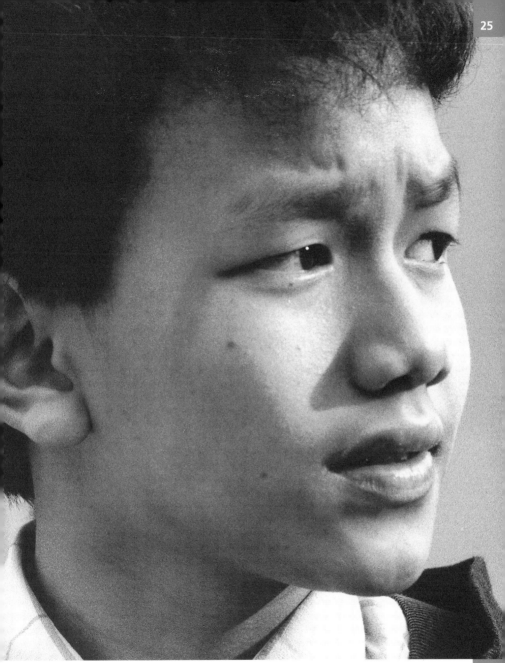

cycles of abuse

There is little doubt that, under certain circumstances, damaged young people can grow up to damage others. Cycles of abuse are *far from inevitable* but they do exist.

AGGRESSION AND VIOLENCE

First, there is a link between abuse in childhood and aggressive violence in adolescence. Physical and sexual abuse are commonly found in the background of violent offenders. How strong is this link? Research (see page 17) suggests that three in four violent young offenders are abused in some way – but this is only one side of the picture. To understand the inter-generational links properly we also need to know *how often* abused young people grow up to become violent. A rather different picture emerges when abused young people are followed into adolescence and beyond. Studies have reported that well over a third of abused males, and perhaps one in eight females, sexually abuse somebody else before reaching the age of eighteen. The numbers are likely to be even greater by adulthood.

Despite a variety of social, cognitive, psychological and psychodynamic explanations for these cyclical patterns, it is not clear why they occur, who is most likely to be affected, and indeed why most male victims of abuse do not become adult offenders. Research has contributed even less to knowledge about the effects of abuse on violence among women. What is agreed, however, is that whatever the connections between early experiences and later behaviour, early intervention is essential if breaking the cycle of abuse is to have any chance of success.

FROM ABUSED CHILD TO ABUSING PARENT?

The notion of a cycle of deprivation, in which some children grow up to repeat the behaviour of their parents, has been popular for a long time. Studies over the last 40 years or so have demonstrated the high levels of disturbance, including cruelty, in the childhoods of both mothers and fathers who are later violent towards their own children. Oliver and Taylor (1971) provide the most striking illustration with the discovery in the 1960s of physical abuse that ran through at least five generations of the same family.

Cycles of abuse are, however, not the norm. Despite varied estimates of the families affected, a 'good guess' might be that up to one in three parents who abuse their children had been damaged themselves. We do not know what proportion of damaged children become damaging parents but it is likely to be considerably less.

What distinguishes families who repeat abusive behaviour from others who do not? Evidence from the early studies suggested, unsurprisingly, that parents facing difficulties in other aspects of their lives were most likely to mistreat their own children. Those of below average ability and from lower socio-economic groups, who had become parents at a young age and had relatively large families, seemed at particular risk. Marital difficulties, social isolation and mental disorders only added to their own and their children's problems, as did the presence of children who were difficult or had special needs. It is likely that much the same kinds of factors make cycles of violence more likely, and certainly more visible, today.

'For years I tried to put it all behind me but as I got older I started to become a monster just like my parents were to me. Mainly I believe what happened to me as a child and not getting any help of any kind resulted in me losing my three children, as I emotionally abused them, although I didn't realise that was what I was doing.'

(National Commission of Inquiry into the Prevention of Child Abuse, 1996)

Personal experiences of abuse may affect parenting behaviour in other non-abusing but damaging ways. A parent may, for instance, become over protective or she might, while offering good physical care, encounter emotional difficulties.

Evidence suggests that survivors of abuse may also *indirectly* affect the risk that their own children will be abused. They may provide greater opportunities for abuse to occur by putting themselves at an emotional – and hence physical – distance from their children, by not having learned how to offer the best protection in potentially threatening situations, and, very significantly, by attracting potentially abusing partners. More positively they may be especially alert to the threat of abuse and therefore particularly vigilant.

'My kids will never go through what I did. They'll know the signs and they'll know they don't have to keep quiet. Nobody is going to take their childhood away from them... I'll see to that, we can see to that.'

(Internet discussion between survivors)

coming through **5**
unscathed

Again and again in the literature there are tantalising suggestions that personal coping strategies can tip the balance between transitory and lasting distress following abuse. Accounts are not fully consistent and rarely can they say with much certainty which characteristics and qualities distinguish well-adjusted from maladjusted young adults. Sometimes, indeed, the answer seems quite elusive:

> *'A 22-year-old woman recalled a childhood marked by emotional coldness, neglect, parental strife, and excessive physical punishment. Over a six-month period, from age 12 to 13 she had to submit to sexual intercourse by her father. Then her parents separated, and she lived with an aunt. She was raped at age 15 by a cousin, and again at age 17 by a boyfriend. She presented herself in the interview as a cheerful, extroverted individual with many friends. She had excellent self-esteem, (and) no sign of depression or neurosis... The only factor we could adduce in her survival was a chronically cheerful and extroverted personality, and her ability to make many friends. Yet this is a* post hoc *interpretation, and exactly why she has survived psychologically is ultimately a mystery.'*
>
> (Bagley, 1995)

It is reassuring to find, too, that some young people and adults who have been abused not only survive but also develop happy, fulfilled and successful personal and public lives.

> *'I believe not only in my ability to survive, but to flourish.'*
>
> (Bain and Sanders, 1990)

Although children have the right to be protected by adults and not held responsible for protecting themselves, any clues about the characteristics or circumstances that aid survival are extremely valuable. Research on resilience to stress and the ability to cope under difficulty is still in its early days, but knowledge is growing. It seems that while each survivor's story is different, a few common themes do stand out.

CHARACTERISTICS OF THE ABUSE

First of all, however, it seems that certain characteristics of abuse are linked to lesser or greater risk of long-term damage. These include:

- **the nature of the abuse:** it is generally believed that young people survive physical abuse better than sexual abuse (although personal accounts sometimes dispute this);

- **the severity of the abuse:** sexual abuse, for instance, seems to have fewer serious and long-lasting effects if physical contact, force and aggression, and penetration, have not been involved;

- **its duration and frequency:** many studies have indicated that better outcomes accompany less frequent abuse, but others have found no consistent association;

- **relationship to the perpetrator:** some studies have suggested that sexual abuse by father figures is particularly damaging; more generally, there are mixed findings on whether outcomes are worse if relatives or non-relatives are involved;

- **age of the perpetrator:** a few studies have suggested less severe outcomes following sexual abuse by an adolescent than by an adult;

- **age when abused:** despite a range of theories, it is unclear whether prepubertal or postpubertal young people are more adversely affected by physical and sexual abuse;

- **sex of the abused person:** it is not possible to say whether males or females are more resilient to abuse as they are rarely compared; most studies of sexual abuse focus on females (most often the victims) or on special populations of males (such as sex offenders) where a high rate of abuse may be found; and

- **the family context:** not surprisingly, some studies have suggested fewer adverse effects of sexual abuse if there is strong family support and if parents encourage disclosure and do not react negatively to the abuse; clearly the situation is complex where a father figure is the suspected perpetrator.

SPEAKING OUT

There seems to be general agreement that acknowledging and speaking out about abuse is the first step in healing damage – provided that the disclosure is positively received.

Many older survivors say they never spoke out because they did not think they would be believed, and feared rejection – and because there did not seem to be anybody to tell. Telephone helplines have made a considerable difference: adult survivors of abuse were the most frequent callers to ChildLine when it was first launched and remain significant contributors of calls to both this and the NSPCC helpline.

THINKING POSITIVE

Personal reports indicate that people who feel in control of their lives, rather than submissive and fatalistic, cope better. These individuals have a more positive self-image and do not feel to blame for what has happened to them. They also tend to be optimistic about the future and do what they can to make sure they do not 'give in' to the stress they have experienced or damage others in a similar way.

There seems to be some disagreement whether distancing oneself from what has happened can be a good coping strategy. For some survivors it seems that it is, while for others who become abusive themselves, dissociation from early experiences means they do not link the pain they felt as children with the misery they inflict on their own children.

Of course there is some circularity involved as young people with high self-esteem, confidence and self-understanding may be less vulnerable to violence in the family – not least because they are most likely to resist and to report physical or sexual assault. Testimonies do nonetheless support the common-sense view that feelings can be as important as – if not more important than – actions for long-term survival.

'I think I got through it because as a child I put in place some good defence mechanisms, forgetting some of the stuff. I know that I forgot it almost as soon as it happened and of course as an adult I'd forgotten the whole thing. It was the defence of not feeling feelings and not feeling physical pain otherwise I don't think I would have survived...'

(Gordon, 1994)

A 'GOOD FRIEND'

There is clear and consistent evidence that good relationships offering good social support help people cope with a wide range of problems and difficulties. These may both protect abused children and young people as they grow up and sustain them in adulthood. It does not seem important who provides support and with what regularity: what matters is that it is enduring and readily available. The main message is that a 'good friend' can reduce the immediate effects of abuse as well as minimise the risk that a cycle of abuse will ensue.

The crucial role of social support in childhood is confirmed by studies looking at the parenting behaviour of abused mothers according to their early experiences of abuse and family relationships. Those growing up with warm, supportive relationships seem least likely to abuse their own children however much abuse they personally suffered.

> *'Without the love and support of my maternal grandparents I would not have survived into an adult; I would have destroyed myself through starvation or an overdose.'*
>
> *(National Commission of Inquiry into the Prevention of Child Abuse, 1996)*

Not only receiving, but also giving, social support appears protective. Helping other people, including brothers and sisters, or even caring for a pet, has been found to aid resistance to stress following abuse.

A SUPPORTIVE PARTNER

A spouse or partner was most likely to be mentioned as their main source of informal help by survivors who wrote to the National Commission of Inquiry into the Prevention of Child Abuse. They were cited as most important by one in three of the 233 respondents who had received such help as compared with friends who were mentioned by only one in twenty five.

Marriage to, or cohabitation with, a survivor of abuse may not be easy. Personal accounts indicate that enormous demands can be put on partners who may need to be not only very supportive but also especially patient, understanding and long-suffering.

Research has consistently shown that a 'good' marriage can be protective in the face of many types

> *'I am hoping that some day I will stop hitting my husband in my sleep. It's not too often now but, he copes well, he understands it's the 'child' fighting him not me.'*
>
> *(National Commission of Inquiry into the Prevention of Child Abuse, 1996)*

of difficulty, but conversely that a 'bad' marriage is not. It is evident that early abuse is among these.

ACHIEVEMENT AND SUCCESS

As self-esteem is tied up with resilience, it is not surprising that research suggests that achievement at school, college or elsewhere is powerful in protecting against the effects of abuse. A high IQ is helpful in this context, both by increasing awareness of potentially abusive situations and by encouraging achievement and success in other spheres.

Achievement need not be in education or employment. Having children of one's own may, for instance, help.

'By far the best thing is watching my children laughing with me and even at me at times and being able to hug them without feeling ill at ease and letting them know I love them and will always be there for them, and, hopefully, by having a loving and open relationship with them I can protect them from systematic abuse like I suffered.'

(National Commission of Inquiry into the Prevention of Child Abuse, 1996)

'Here began the struggle, you see,

   between this little child and me.

For she had to be quiet and remain inside,

   so her guilt and shame I could hide.

Now someone has told her she wasn't to blame;

   and there wasn't a reason for her to feel shame.'

(Hall and Lloyd, 1989)

support and treatment **6**

The damaging experiences discussed throughout this Fact File take many forms and have very varied outcomes. Just what leads to what, and when and why, is frequently unclear. As a result, there is no single or simple way to intervene to prevent abuse, reduce the effects of damage in the short-term, alleviate the stress faced by survivors in later years, or minimise the chances that damage in one generation will be linked to damage in the next.

A number of main prevention and intervention tasks can, nonetheless, be identified in relation to children, young people and families in general as well as the abused, their families, and the perpetrators. This section begins by listing these, and continues by describing some of the most important strategies for meeting them, and outlining the main contributions of statutory, private, voluntary and 'informal' services.

THE MAIN TASKS

A primary goal of services should be to prevent abuse and the suffering it creates. Treatment in a more formal sense should be available to deal with difficulties it has not been possible to prevent. Although by no means an exhaustive list, there are perhaps six particularly important tasks of all such support and intervention to assist children and young adults avoid or survive damage occurring in childhood:

- ▪ *understanding and acknowledging abuse:* the recent and widespread recognition that child abuse really exists does not seem to have led to a reduction in the problem – indeed child abuse has become ever more visible; however it has increased awareness of the 'signs' of abuse, it has helped survivors to speak out, and it has encouraged the development of more appropriate support and services. Even greater understanding and acknowledgement of abuse and its effects is however still needed;

- ▪ *supporting young families 'at risk':* services for young families can help to prevent child abuse by offering support in times of stress, by identifying potentially abusive situations at an early stage, and by supporting parents who were themselves victims of child abuse to ensure that cycles of damage are not set in motion;

- ▪ *helping abused children and their families in the short-term:* identifying abuse, protecting children from its recurrence, offering support and treatment to family members, and helping the family to get back 'on its feet', can do much to reduce long-term damage;

- **providing support for older 'survivors':** many young adults who suffered abuse in childhood and have difficulty coming to terms with their experiences can be helped by support and understanding;

- **treating the perpetrators:** the risk of abuse and re-abuse of children and young people is reduced if perpetrators can in some way be prevented from re-offending; and

- **minimising the risk of cycles of damage:** two ways of reducing cycles of abuse are (i) to prevent victims (usually young males) embarking on a career of violent abuse themselves, and (ii) to support victims of violence in parenthood to ensure they do not treat their own children as they were treated themselves.

FORMS OF PREVENTION AND INTERVENTION

Help and support for those at risk of, or involved in some way with, abuse can mean many things ranging from a listening ear at one extreme to extensive and intensive therapy at the other. They may be offered informally by family or friends, semi-formally by volunteers or 'mentors', or formally by professional services. They may aim to reduce anxiety and distress, change attitudes and/or behaviour, or just offer friendship and support. Children, adolescents or adults – or families as a whole – can be involved, and 'help' may be given on a one-to-one or a group basis. Everybody's problems are individual and so are their solutions.

It is not possible here to describe exactly what different approaches to intervention entail. One or more of the following basic and overlapping strategies is, however, likely to be involved.

'There is no "one size fits all" treatment model or protocol, and we should be sceptical of either self-help or professionally led programmes that suggest otherwise.'

(Briere and others, 1996)

Counselling

Counselling is an umbrella term which refers to talking to children, young people, their families and others about abuse in order to help resolve difficulties. Among its tasks are:

- **encouraging disclosure of abuse – and talking about it:** acknowledging and being open about abusive experiences is generally recognised to be the first step in recovering from damage;

- **helping the victim come to terms with the abuse:** stress counselling may be appropriate either in the short-term following abuse or much later where childhood trauma remains unresolved; this can deal with emotional effects, help the young person understand what has happened, encourage appropriate thinking about sexuality, and try to make sure that young people (usually boys) do not become abusers in their turn;

- **helping other family members:** parents who feel they are at risk of abusing (or re-abusing) their children may need support as may those who find it difficult to accept that another member of the family has abused their children; siblings need help if they have also been abused or if they blame their sister/brother for breaking up their family; and

- **dealing with additional problems facing the family:** families may need help not only to cope with abuse but also to deal with alcohol and drug misuse, marital difficulties, unemployment – or whatever may be affecting family members and contributing to household stress.

This form of support is offered by a range of professionals or lay volunteers, or through telephone helplines. It may be offered routinely once abuse has been detected, or it may be available on request through school counsellors and others.

Therapy

There is not always a clear line between therapy and counselling, although the former usually refers to treatment provided by a therapist, psychologist or psychiatrist according to a specific model or theoretical framework. In general, the goals of therapy are to enable the client to regain control over his or her life and emotions by dealing with internal conflicts and unresolved traumas that are creating behaviour and personality disorders, and to understand more about personal feelings and actions. Often the notion of confronting and re-experiencing trauma is central.

Therapy is delivered in two main ways – to individuals or in a group setting. It is argued that a one-to-one approach enables a close and trusting relationship to develop between the therapist and survivor. Although this may lead to over-dependence, it makes it easier for treatment to focus on an individual's problems and proceed at a suitable pace. It is also more confidential and can be less threatening to the survivor who lacks confidence and may feel overwhelmed and excluded in a group situation. Group therapy, on the other hand, can overcome social isolation by enabling survivors to realise they are not alone and allowing them to share their experiences and learn from others. It can also be used to help members of the same family resolve their interpersonal difficulties.

Young people as well as adults may be offered formal therapy. Those with serious psychological or behavioural problems may require a prolonged therapeutic programme, possibly as an in-patient

> *'Caution: There's a Child Inside...*
>
> *There is a child inside me, and though she's very small,*
>
> *There was a time not long ago she seemed not there at all.*
>
> *Then one day I was asked to tell a little of my past.*
>
> *As I spoke and walls came down, a little comfort the child had found.*
>
> *Hiding no longer would keep her content, though protecting her had been my intent.'*
>
> *(Hall and Lloyd, 1989)*

Behaviour and Skills Training

Trying to change behaviour or teach new skills is an important aspect of intervention for surviving abuse. Indeed it may be a component of counselling or therapy. The many ways in which this can be done include:

- **encouraging children and young people to avoid abuse:** preventive educational programmes try to help young people to recognise, and remove themselves from, situations where they might be 'at risk';

- **providing young people with strategies to deal with abuse:** these programmes also try to teach strategies to avoid situations where abuse may recur;

- **working with victims of abuse:** a range of approaches has been adopted including, for example, helping survivors deal with their emotions and memories, and encouraging appropriate sexual attitudes and behaviour;

■ **_developing self-esteem:_** helping young people recognise that being abused was not their fault and does not mean they need always be a 'victim' can boost morale and assist in dealing with later problems; programmes of this kind may not address abuse directly but work on activities the young person does well – such as dancing or acting – and can be rewarded for;

■ **_parenting programmes:_** most young people become parents in their turn and can benefit from learning how to bring up their children without abusing or damaging them; parenting skills may be taught to broad groups of young adults or focused on those at risk of abusing their own children; and

■ **_working with the perpetrators:_** preventing children and young people who have been abused from becoming abusers themselves is an important focus of intervention, and a range of behavioural techniques have been used with potential adolescent sexual offenders to prevent them abusing or re-abusing other young people.

Family Support

Long-term research on physical abuse in particular suggests that family support and family circumstances are crucial in protecting children against longer-term abuse. There has, nonetheless, been recent concern that child protection and family support have far too often been seen as distinct activities for different groups of people rather than complementary parts of an integrated service provision.

There are many ways in which family support can help to alleviate pressures on families, encourage more effective parenting, and hence reduce the risk of child abuse. This support may involve counselling in a general sense, or it may mean practical assistance such as day care for small children, toy libraries, drop-in stress centres, home-school link programmes, or any other community initiative that might enable families to function more effectively. A recent Department of Health document argues strongly for a 're-focusing' of child protection work to include much more emphasis on support of these kinds.

Treatment of Perpetrators

A rather different way of helping young people to survive abuse is to prevent that abuse in the first place – and that involves the measures taken against perpetrators.

The first issue is whether either incarceration or treatment or both is best. The efficacy and desirability of simply locking abusers up _without treatment_ is questioned – apart from the benefits of taking them out of circulation for a period of time – as

studies have indicated that spending time in prison, often with other convicted abusers, may reinforce abusive behaviour patterns through repetitious fantasising about abusive acts. On the other hand, while treatment does seem to be effective in reducing subsequent abuse among children and young people, particularly if started early, its value is less clear for adult multiple abusers.

A further dilemma arises when convicted abusers have completed a spell in prison and are released into the community. How can children and young people be protected if the behaviour of adult abusers is hard to change? The recent Sex Offender Register is an initiative that tries to resolve this problem.

According to the Sex Offenders Act 1997, anybody convicted or cautioned for paedophile or other serious sexual offences who fails to notify their changes of name and address to the Police is committing a criminal offence. The Police may pass any information they receive on to local schools or youth groups, or even individuals, if they consider that the person poses a threat. Despite concerns about vigilante action, the positive effects of this legislation remain to be seen.

WHO OFFERS WHAT?

Collaboration and co-operation within the statutory agencies and between statutory and voluntary bodies, as well as some overlap in function, makes it difficult to specify exactly who provides what. Some indication of the main responsibilities of the various agencies are, however, outlined below.

The Role of Statutory Agencies

A large number of statutory agencies are, in some way or another, involved in helping young people to survive damage from abuse. Their roles are, in brief, as follows:

Social services departments

The Children Act 1989 places the responsibility to protect children and young people from significant harm with a range of agencies and gives three agencies – social services departments as well as the Police and the NSPCC – special powers to investigate and intervene in cases of abuse. Social workers (some of whom have a specialist child protection role) will generally take the lead when child abuse is suspected by making an appropriate referral, ensuring that the child is safe in the short-term, making an initial assessment of the situation and needs, calling a child protection conference, and deciding whether the child's name should be placed on the Child Protection Register. More detailed assessments and appropriate intervention follow, including the possibility of removing the young person from the family home or encouraging an adult to leave. The case is later followed up and, when appropriate, the child's name is removed from the Register. Social services departments have responsibility for managing both child protection conferences and the Child Protection Register.

Social service departments are often responsible for organising day–care services such as nurseries, play groups, out–of–school clubs and holiday schemes, and childminders. All the staff of these services offer potential help and support by recognising and referring cases of abuse as well as by relieving parents of the stress of full-time child care.

The Police

As one of the three agencies with special powers to intervene in cases of abuse, the Police alone are able to provide a child with a place of protection by removing him or her from home without an application to the court. More generally, the Police become involved in cases of child abuse where a crime may have been committed and there is a need to identify the perpetrator, collect vital evidence, and take a decision on whether or not to press charges.

The education service

Education services play a central role in child protection as teachers, assistants, education welfare officers, school nurses and educational psychologists working in nurseries, schools and other educational establishments are ideally placed to identify abuse and refer children and young people to the appropriate agencies. The Department for Education and Employment has set out how all staff should be alert to signs of abuse and know how to report concerns or suspicions. Schools and colleges should be aware of the child protection procedures established by the Area Child Protection Committee and designate an appropriately-trained member of staff to co-ordinate action within the institution and with other agencies including the ACPC. They should also have their own procedures in the event of any instance of suspected abuse, and each local education authority should have a senior officer responsible for co-ordinating action on child protection across the authority.

Under the Children Act 1989, social services departments must inform schools if a pupil is named on the Child Protection Register, and education authorities have the responsibility to co-operate with other agencies and, in particular, to assist social services departments when allegations of abuse have been made.

Schools and further education establishments also have an important role to play in preventing abuse through the curriculum – such as by teaching young people to resist abuse and preparing them for responsible parenthood – although the extent to which they do this through personal and social education courses is variable. They may also play a protective role through providing counsellors who may or may not be teachers. Peer support schemes can, in addition, be important in this context.

Health services

The many sections of the health services to play a role include:

- midwives and health visitors who work together in identifying families who might be at risk, promoting good relationships between parents and baby, and supporting parents with young children;

- all hospital staff, and especially those in accident and emergency departments, who need to be alert to signs of child abuse and liaise with others in the case of suspected child injury;

- health visitors, doctors and community paediatricians at child health clinics who play an important part in identifying abuse and offering treatment;

- child and adolescent mental health services which have a number of roles in this area including: identifying and referring abuse; assessment of, and treatment for, families in which abuse has occurred; and direct work with young abusers;

■ adult mental health services, including psychological and psychiatric services, which may offer treatment for adult survivors referred either for a history of abuse or for more general psychological problems; and

■ GPs (and practice nurses) who are likely to have the most prolonged contact with individual families. Again, their role is to identify abuse, refer cases appropriately, and liaise with other professionals and agencies in offering suitable help and support.

The Probation Service

The Probation Service is the primary criminal justice agency working with convicted sex offenders of all types aged 16 years or above. As well as supervising and offering treatment for sex offenders, either directly or in partnership with other agencies, probation officers supervise and monitor many of the most dangerous sex offenders in the community (including those who deny their offending or are not motivated to change their behaviour). These responsibilities are carried out by assessing and reviewing levels of risk, need and motivation. The risk is then managed largely

through close liaison and co-operation with other agencies which share the responsibility for offering treatment and protecting potential victims.

More generally, the Probation Service is frequently involved in child protection work in the course of family courts proceedings and through its supervision of offenders, and has well established child protection and risk management procedures. Children of offenders are often at high risk of being targeted by sex offenders because their parents are in difficulties and susceptible to grooming by perpetrators.

In recent years the Probation Service has also become involved in more direct work with victims of violent and sexual crimes. It also works more with families experiencing domestic violence. Group work programmes are being established with both abusers and their families. This is particularly important given the increasing evidence that the experience of domestic violence as a child may predate sexually abusive behaviour in adulthood.

Voluntary Agencies

The voluntary sector, which works alongside and collaboratively with statutory services, represents an umbrella of organisations and agencies which vary considerably in size, location (e.g. national or local), aims and objectives, approach to intervention and, importantly, resources. Almost all voluntary agencies working with children are likely to find themselves offering support to victims of abuse through one or other of their services, and most of the major voluntary child care organisations provide specific therapeutic and support services to abuse victims and their families.

Most of these agencies are required to refer children 'at risk' of significant harm to statutory agencies, and the NSPCC is alone in having the power to apply for care, supervision and child assessment orders in its own right. This charitable organisation has a long tradition of employing social workers to identify and prevent cruelty to children and is, more and more, working with local authorities in developing child protection teams and projects to provide specialist services. Nationally, it also provides training and offers a free child protection helpline open to all.

Another important national voluntary organisation is ChildLine which also provides free 24-hour telephone helplines – mainly for children but also for adults and parents including adult survivors. In the year to the end of March 1996, contact was made with at least 16,000 children and some 800 adults talking about their own experiences of physical and sexual abuse. In reporting on their work over the first ten years, they note that whereas 80 per cent of children who phoned in 1986–7 said they had not previously disclosed their sexual abuse to anyone, this proportion had dropped to 47 per cent by 1995–6. The comparative figures for the disclosure of physical abuse were 80 and 19 per cent.

Exploring Parenthood is another national organisation to provide advice and counselling through a national telephone helpline – although, in this case, for parents. It also runs group programmes for families under stress, and offers training for agencies wishing to provide parental skills education, including those involved in crime prevention and community safety programmes.

Alongside voluntary organisations set up to deal with difficulties specifically relating to abuse are others with a more general remit such as Alcoholics Anonymous or the Samaritans. These may be the first point of contact for survivors if the symptom of damage (alcoholism or suicidal tendencies) rather than its cause (earlier abuse) that prompts the self-referral.

Details of many voluntary agencies working with survivors are provided at the end of the Fact File.

Private Services

Private services tend to run parallel to statutory – and sometimes voluntary – services and differ largely in the greater speed and availability with which they are offered to those who can afford them. Private nurseries and play groups, private schools and private health care, for instance, fulfil similar functions to their statutory equivalents and hence have a comparable role to play in helping young people to survive damage.

Therapy and counselling are not widely available through the statutory services and, where they do exist, may be restricted to a limited number of sessions after a long wait. Private services do, therefore, fulfil a need in this area for those willing and able to pay.

Volunteer and Befriender Schemes

There has been a marked growth in volunteer and befriending schemes over recent years. The advantages of these are that they tend to be less stigmatising, and hence preferable, to more formal services, and that they are free.

A good example of a befriender scheme is Home-Start which, according to the guidance accompanying the Children Act 1989, can 'offer parents under stress significant amounts of time from volunteers who are likely to be seen as friends with no power or tradition of interfering in family life and who may themselves have surmounted similar difficulties'. The scheme, which has been operating in the UK for more than 20 years, focuses on families with pre-school children, and works alongside statutory services in providing support for a range of difficulties including suspected child abuse. It works through a network of autonomous home visiting schemes reaching around one thousand pre–school children a year.

Another example is NEWPIN which has been operating nationally for almost 20 years to prevent damaged parents bringing up damaged children. In this scheme, mothers are matched with befrienders who help them to reduce their stress and distress and develop good relationships with their children. Later, these mothers may join a therapeutic support group and, in addition, undertake training to enable them to become befrienders in their turn. NEWPIN is also cited in guidance to the Children Act 1989 as a good example of how to help parents feel less isolated and develop better parenting skills.

Other Special Projects

There are many examples of special projects working with families considered at risk of damage and abuse across the country as a whole. Most of these focus on developing family relationships and parenting skills and are fairly local and small-scale. Different techniques are used – including counselling, group therapy, behaviour modification – and the programmes last for varying lengths of time. In most projects the participating families are referred by statutory agencies. Some may receive local authority funding.

Self-help

There is no fixed prescription for self-help and it might mean picking up a useful book, phoning a helpline, visiting a survivors' web site on the Internet (see *personal accounts and self–help,* page 59), consulting a GP, talking to friends and asking their advice, making an appointment with a therapist – or even writing a letter or a book.

Another possibility is to join a self-help group. These – sometimes called victim support groups – are one of the main forms of help for older survivors of abuse and damage. Although many are developed by statutory or voluntary agencies, very often they are instigated and run by survivors themselves. Overall they serve a number of functions including providing relatively informal venues for survivors to 'drop in' at on a regular or irregular basis, trying to help

'As I write this I am smiling and crying... smiling because I am proud of myself and crying because I had to go through so much to get this anyway.'

(National Commission of Inquiry into the Prevention of Child Abuse, 1996)

individuals understand more about abuse and its consequences, or campaigning for legislative change and increased public education.

Although it is difficult to evaluate the effectiveness of self-help groups, the fact that they tend to be well-attended is proof in itself of their value. Participation is free, voluntary and non-stigmatising, and problems can be shared with others in similar situations. Survivors, moreover, are to some extent in control of their own treatment. On the other hand, however, they are unable to deal with severe symptoms or problems that need professional attention, and their structure and content is highly dependent on the individual participants.

Recent years have seen the development of new sources of information, support and advice which have increased the possibilities of self-help for survivors of abuse – even if these remain inadequate to meet the full extent and complexity of need. For example:

■ the BBC Support Services have put together a *Survivors Directory* containing hundreds of national and local contact addresses and phone numbers of groups working on issues of sexual violence;

■ Directory and Book Services (DABS) have produced a *National Resource Directory* with descriptions of over 300 organisations in England, Scotland and Wales concerned with recovery from, and prevention of, child sexual abuse;

■ survivor groups have been introduced onto the Internet and include discussion groups through which survivors can communicate by e-mail; and

■ there are currently moves to establish a National Association for People Abused in Childhood as a national umbrella group for survivors; this aims to establish a national information line and postal service for people requiring advice and information about help available to overcome childhood abuse, to provide support, training, information and resources to persons and organisations supporting people who have experienced ill treatment and/or neglect in childhood, and to raise public awareness of the continuing impact of child abuse in adulthood.

More details on these initiatives are given at the end of the Fact File.

a task for us all 7

The main conclusion of this Fact File is that child abuse is a serious problem which results in considerable misery and can prevent normal social and emotional growth in young adulthood and beyond. There is at present no single and reliable solution although a number of strategies and approaches do appear helpful in reducing damage. Limited resources and availability, however, mean that these are not widely accessible.

Preventing abuse and helping survivors should, nonetheless, be a priority. Disregarding the problems involved is a false economy as it is much more expensive to deal with the family difficulties and breakdown, the depression and mental health problems, the delinquency and violence, the drug addiction and alcoholism, and the widespread distress that may otherwise result.

An enormous step forward has been taken by the increase in public knowledge and understanding of child abuse over recent years. This has not caused the problem to go away but it has reduced the stigma, encouraged survivors to speak out, and led to more and better help and support. Yet there is much further to go. Shortcomings and gaps in provision remain, and we do not know enough about the forms of prevention, intervention and support that work best. More understanding of the impact of statutory bodies such as social services departments, or voluntary agencies like the NSPCC, who are major service providers in this area, would also be helpful. It is not easy to demonstrate the effectiveness of interventions, but the more that we know the better we will be able to reduce the lasting effects of early abuse.

'Now forty–seven years later with a broken marriage behind me, living in poverty, I feel no hope for the future as I feel I have not got a future, even as I write this letter. My mind is a complete shambles. I find I can't cope through life because I never got any help, time has passed me by and it feels too late – the emotional scars never heal no matter how long.'

(National Commission of Inquiry into the Prevention of Child Abuse, 1996)

There is also much more that could be done for those who endure the long-term effects of early damage. Of the over one thousand survivors of abuse who wrote to the National Commission of Inquiry into the Prevention of Child Abuse, 44 per cent said they had received no formal help at any time and more than a quarter said that nothing, whether formal or informal help, had been useful. The feeling conveyed by these letters was certainly one of considerable unmet need.

Formal services are under-resourced – and are likely to be for the foreseeable future – and few are available to adult survivors. Statutory agencies, such as social services

departments, offer little to this group who are more likely to benefit from volunteer and befriending schemes or self-help. Children and families tend to receive a more comprehensive service because there is a statutory obligation for specified agencies to intervene in all cases of suspected child abuse. Nonetheless survivors appear appreciative of any formal or informal support they do get and, conversely, usually say that matters are made worse when they receive none.

What can be done to improve matters without enormous financial implications? Three important priorities would seem to be:

- to promote greater public understanding of the nature and wide-ranging effects of serious abuse occurring in childhood;

- to encourage more survivors of abuse to come forward and speak out; and

- to make sure that information, advice and support are available when they do.

These tasks fall to us all. Politicians should give proper priority to the problems involved, practitioners provide the appropriate services, and the media educate responsibly. And, whether we are abused ourselves, at risk of causing abuse, or simply a bystander, we have an important role to play in doing what we can to share problems and difficulties and to contribute to a reduction in the stigma and damage caused by abuse. As the recent Community Care and ChildLine campaign has highlighted, child protection is everybody's business.

We will have succeeded only when everyone's experience reflects the words of the survivor who said:

> *'You don't have to be a victim for ever more. You can do more than just cope. It is possible to survive, to live... Never forget that good things can come out of adversity. Survival is an attainable goal.'*
>
> *(Rouf, 1996)*

some key books, 8
articles and reports

Bagley, C. (1995)
Child Sexual Abuse and Mental Health in Adolescents and Adults.
Avebury.

Beitchman, J.H. and others (1991)
A review of the short-term effects of child sexual abuse. Child Abuse and Neglect, vol. 15, pp. 537–556.

Beitchman, J.H. and others (1992)
A review of the long-term effects of child sexual abuse. Child Abuse and Neglect, vol. 16, pp. 101–118.

Bibby, P.C. (ed) (1996)
Organised Abuse. The Current Debate.
Arena.

Boswell, G. (1995)
Violent Victims. The Prevalence of Abuse and Loss in the Lives of Section 53 Offenders,
The Prince's Trust and the Royal Jubilee Trusts.

Briere, J. N. (1992)
Child Abuse Trauma: Theory and Treatment of the Lasting Effects.
Sage.

Briere, J. and others (eds) (1996)
The APSAC Handbook on Child Maltreatment. [American Professional Society on the Abuse of Children.]
Sage.

Buchanan, A. (1996)
Cycles of Child Maltreatment. Facts, Fallacies and Interventions.
Wiley.

ChildLine (1996)
Talking with Children about Child Abuse: ChildLine's First Ten Years.

Creighton, S. (1992)
Child Abuse Trends in England and Wales 1988–1990. And an overview from 1973–1990.
NSPCC.

Department of Health (1995)
Child Protection Messages from Research.
HMSO.

Department of Health (1997)
Children and Young People on Child Protection Registers, Year Ending 31 March 1996.
HMSO.

Elliott, M. (ed) (1993)
Female Sexual Abuse of Children: The Ultimate Taboo.
Longman.

Ferguson, H., Gilligan, R., and Torode, R. (1993)
Surviving Childhood Adversity: Issues For Policy and Practice.
Social Studies Press.

Fonagy, P. and others (1994)
The theory and practice of resilience, Journal of Child Psychology and Psychiatry, vol. 35, no. 2, pp. 231–257.

Gough, D. (1993)
Child Abuse Interventions: A Review of the Research Literature.
HMSO.

Hall, L. and Lloyd, S. (1989)
Surviving Child Sexual Abuse: A Handbook for Helping Women Challenge their Past.
Falmer Press.

Home Office, Department of Health, Department of Education and Science, and Welsh Office (1991)
Working Together Under the Children Act 1989: A Guide to Arrangements for Inter-agency Co-operation for the Protection of Children from Abuse.
HMSO.

Howing, P.T. and others (1993)
Maltreatment and the School-Age Child: Developmental Outcomes and System Issues.
The Haworth Press.

Katz, M. (1997)
On Playing a Poor Hand Well: Insights From the Lives of Those who Have Overcome Childhood Risks and Adversities.
WW Norton.

Kelly, L. (1988)
Surviving Sexual Violence.
Polity Press.

Kendall-Tackett, K. and others (1993)
Impact of sexual abuse on children: a review and synthesis of recent empirical studies. Psychological Bulletin, vol. 113, pp. 164–180.

MacLeod, M. (1995)
What Children Tell ChildLine About Being Abused.
ChildLine.

MacLeod, M. (1997)
Child Protection: Everybody's Business.
ChildLine.

Morrison, T., and others (1994)
Sexual Offending Against Children: Assessment and Treatment of Male Abusers.
Routledge.

National Commission of Inquiry into the Prevention of Child Abuse (1996)
Childhood Matters: vol 1, The Report, and vol 2, Background Papers.
Stationery Office.

Oliver, J.E. and Taylor, A. (1971)
Five generations if ill-treated children in one family pedigree. British Journal of Psychiatry, vol. 119, pp. 473–480.

Prentky, R. and Burgess, A.W. (1990)
Rehabilitation of child molesters: a cost-benefit analysis. American Journal of Orthopsychiatry, vol. 60, no. 1, pp. 108–117.

Sanderson, C. (1990)
Counselling Adult Survivors of Child Sexual Abuse.
Jessica Kingsley.

Thompson, R.A. (1995)
Preventing Child Maltreatment Through Social Support.
Sage.

Walker, M. (1992)
Surviving Secrets: The Experience of Abuse for the Child, the Adult and the Helper.
Open University Press.

Wilson, K. and James, A. (1995)
The Child Protection Handbook.
Bailliere Tindall.

personal accounts and **9**
self-help

Ainscough, C. and Toon, K. (1993)
Breaking Free: Help for Survivors of Child Sexual Abuse.
Sheldon Press.

Bain, O. and Sanders, M. (1990)
Out in the Open: A Guide for Young People Who Have Been Sexually Abused.
Virago.

Bass, E. and Davis, L. (1993)
Beginning to Heal: A First Book for Survivors of Child Sexual Abuse.
Cedar.
(Looks at the healing process: remembering, telling someone, grieving and so on. Also contains personal accounts by women who were sexually abused.)

Bass, E. and others (1991)
I Never Told Anyone: Writings by Women Survivors of Child Sexual Abuse.
Harper Perennial.

Ben (1991)
Things in my Head.
Glendale.

Bray, M. (1991)
Poppies on the Rubbish Heap: Sexual Abuse: The Child's Voice.
Canongate Press.
(An independent social worker, founder of Sexual Abuse: Child Consultancy Services, describes the development of her work and techniques, including play therapy. Six case studies of sexually abused children and their outcomes are included.)

Courtney, C.A. (1991)
Morphine and Dolly Mixtures.
Penguin.
(An autobiographical account of a young girl's attempt to protect herself and her siblings from physical and emotional abuse by their father in the 1950's.)

Davis, L. (1991)
Allies in Healing: When the Person You Love was Sexually Abused as a Child.
Harper Perennial.

Elliott, M. and others (1995)
Child sexual abuse prevention: what offenders tell us. Child Abuse & Neglect, vol. 19, no. 5. pp. 579–594.
(Ninety–one sex offenders were interviewed about the methods they used to target children, the age range of their victims, how they selected children and maintained them as victims, and the suggestions they had for preventing sexual abuse.)

Fay (1989)
Listen to Me: Talking Survival.
Gatehouse Project.
(The author presents a personal account of child sexual abuse by her brothers, her depression, survival into a long-term relationship, motherhood and support from a women's group.)

Fever, F. (1994)
Who Cares? Memories of a Childhood in Barnardo's.
Warner.

Fraser, S., and Chalmers, C. (1992)
A Helping Hand? *Scottish Child*,
(Feb/Mar). pp. 22–25.
(A victim of sexual abuse recounts the experience of being abused and its aftermath.)

Galey, I. (1989)
I Couldn't Cry when Daddy Died.
Settle Press.
(The autobiography of a woman who was sexually abused by her father until he committed suicide when she was 14.)

Golding, V.
Speaking Out Leads to Survival. *Social Work Today*, vol. 21, no. 28 (31 May).
pp. 18–19.
(Personal account of a girl sexually abused by her step-father.)

Gordon, P. (1994)
I Could Never Tell Anyone: Personal Testimonies of Sexual Abuse.
BBC Education

Grubman-Black, S.D. (1990)
Broken Boys / Mending Men: Recovery fromChildhood Sexual Abuse.
TAB books.
(A comprehensive account of how boys survive childhood sexual abuse. Personal stories tell of withdrawal, isolation, and loss of self esteem, and how society's view of what it is to be male hinders their recovery.)

Hall, L. and Lloyd, S. (1993)
Surviving Child Sexual Abuse: A Handbook for Helping Women Challenge their Past.
Falmer Press.

Kelly, B. (1990)
A Moment's Grace. *Social Work Today*, vol. 22, no. 15 (6 Dec). pp. 17–18.
(Two offenders relate their experiences at the Gracewell Clinic, the first independent treatment centre for sex offenders in Britain.)

Kirk, P. (1994)
A Survivor Myself: Experiences of Child Abuse.
Yorkshire Art Circus.
(First person accounts by ten adults abused as children.)

Landry, D.B. (1991)
Family Fallout: A Handbook for Families of Adult Sexual Abuse Survivors.
Safer Society Press.

Lew, M. (1988)
Victims No Longer: men recovering from incest and other sexual child abuse.
Nevraumont Publishing.

Malone, C. and others (1996)
The Memory Bird: survivors of sexual abuse.
Virago.
(An anthology of contributions from survivors of sexual abuse. Besides giving expression to the recurring themes of anger, pain, confrontation and responsibility, the book also offers evidence of survivors'resilience, hope and strength.)

Meadow, R. (1990)
120 years on: Voices on Child Abuse. *British Medical Journal,* vol. 301, no. 6754 (3 Oct). pp. 714–716.
(Various personal accounts of people involved in child abuse cases.)

Miller, A. (1990)
Banished Knowledge: Facing Childhood Injuries. [Translated from the German by Leila Vennewitz.]
Virago.
(The author describes how, having rejected psychoanalysis, she found a therapy to help her resolve her childhood traumas.)

Morris, S. and Wheatley, H. (1994)
Time to Listen: The Experiences of Young People in Foster and Residential Care.
ChildLine.
(Describes calls to ChildLine by 676 children in foster or residential care, as well as face to face interviews with another 63. The young people tell what it is like to be in public care, pinpoint the problems and make practical recommendations for improvements.)

Napier, N.J. (1994)
Getting Through the Day: Strategies For Adults Hurt as Children.
Norton.

Pembroke, L.R. (ed.) (1994)
Self Harm: Perspectives from Personal Experience.
Survivors Speak Out.
(Argues that self-harm is a painful but understandable response to distress, particularly in western culture, and that self-harm thrives in an environment where people are stripped of freedom and control over their lives and yet are expected to behave in a controlled manner.)

Prescott, E. (1996)
Mondays are Yellow, Sundays are Grey: A Mother's Fight to Save her Children from the Nightmare of Sexual Abuse.
Women's Press.

Rouf, K. (1988)
Mousie.
Children's Society.
(Story for young children about sexual abuse emphasising the right to tell and be believed.)

Rouf, K. (1989)
Journey Through Darkness: The Path from Victim to Survivor. *Educational and Child Psychology,* vol. 6, no. 1. pp. 6–10. (Special issue.)
(A personal account of a daughter's sexual abuse by her father.)

Rouf, K. (1989)
Secrets.
Children's Society.
(Cartoon-strip story for older children about child sexual abuse within the family emphasising the child's right to tell and be believed.)

Rouf, K. (1991)
Into Pandora's Box.
Children's Society.
(Poems written by a survivor of child sexual abuse describing her feelings – rage, depression, guilt – towards her father the perpetrator, her mother, social workers, and psychologists.)

Safe & Sound (1995)
So Who Are We Meant to Trust Now? Responding to Abuse in Care: The Experiences of Young People.
National Society for Prevention of Cruelty to Children.
(Report detailing the experiences of young people in care who were abused by the professionals responsible for them. The young people tried to alert those in authority to the abuse and are extremely critical of the way their complaints were dealt with.)

Sonkin, D.J. (1992)
Wounded Boys, Heroic Men: a man's guide to recovering from child abuse.
Longmeadow Press.

Smith, R. (1989)
Jeanette Roberts: caring is the cure.
Foster Care, no. 59. pp. 12–14.
(A personal account of a woman's childhood experience of sexual abuse and how she grew through it to become the foster parent of over 40 children with similar experiences.)

Stafford, J.M. (1990)
Light in the Dust.
Trustline Publishing.
(An autobiographical account of sexual abuse in a working class family in Staffordshire. Vividly sets the experience of abuse in the context of poverty, unemployment and maternal ill health. Follows the story to later repercussions in adulthood.)

Stanley, C. (ed) (1994)
I Could Never Tell Anyone: Experiences of Being Abused as a Child in the First Half of the Century.
BBC Education.

Walker, M. (1992)
Surviving Secrets: The Experience of Abuse for the Child, the Adult and the Helper.
Open University Press.
(Based on interviews with adult survivors of child abuse who talk about their experiences and the effectiveness of treatment.)

SELF-HELP AND INFORMATION ON THE INTERNET

There are a large number of sites on the Internet offering information and advice for survivors of abuse. Sites may belong to official, well-known organisations or to individuals whose authority and expertise is less easy to assess. At the time of writing, a simple search using 'abuse' and 'survivor' on the *Yahoo* search site produced 74 site matches. Some may be transient but others are being added daily. Sites may simply offer information or they may be interactive with users who can exchange written accounts or communciate by e-mail. As with many of the Internet sources, their value and authority must be a matter for personal judgement. However, the number of visitors to the site example offered here – 47,828 in 18 months – indicates their growing significance.

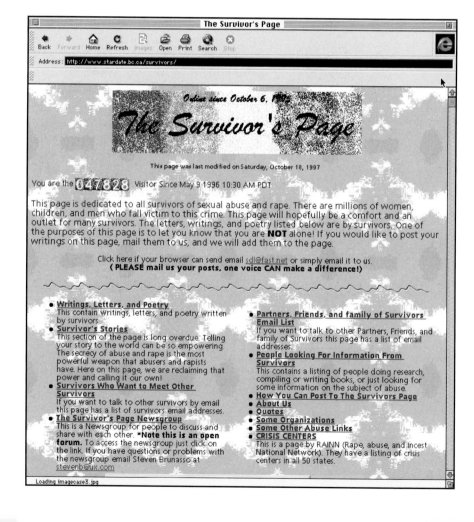

organisations for **10**
survivors

The following list, which is not exhaustive, indicates a range of organisations which may provide help or information for survivors of sexual abuse. Fuller details of local and national support services in Britain and Ireland can be obtained from the *'Survivors Directory'* (Broadcasting Support Services) or the *DABS National Resource Directory (Directory and Book Services)* (see entries below).

ACCURACY ABOUT ABUSE
PO Box 3125
London NW3 5QB
Tel: 0171 431 5339
Fax: 0171 433 3101
Contact: Marjorie Orr
(Set up to counter misinformation in the public mind about child abuse; a campaigning group which aims to disseminate information to the media, to mental professionals, and in legal/ political circles.)

ACTION AGAINST CHILD SEXUAL ABUSE
PO Box 9502
London N17 7BW
Tel: 0181 365 9382
(Publishes Action Against Child Sexual Abuse *newsletter.)*

ALCOHOLICS ANONYMOUS
General Service Office
PO Box 1
Stonebow House, Stonebow
York, North Yorkshire, YO1 2NJ
Tel: 01904 644026
    0171 352 3001 **(helpline)**
(Provides support for people with difficulties involving alcohol, including survivors of abuse.)

BEACON FOUNDATION
Tel: 01745 343600
(available 10.00 am-4pm)
(Telephone helpline for survivors of ritual abuse and those working with them.)

BREAKFREE
The Breakfree Centre
11 Bailgate
Lincoln
Tel: 01522 543 100
(Counsels adult survivors of childhood sexual abuse.)

BREAKTHROUGH FOR YOUTH LIMITED
64 Brendon
Laindon
Essex, SS15 5XL
Tel: 01268 417 355
Fax: 01268 417 355
(Publishes 'Caring for children and young people who have been sexually abused', a video resource pack.)

BRISTOL CRISIS SERVICE FOR WOMEN
Tel: 0117 925 1119
(helpline: Friday and Saturday 9pm–12.30am)
(Specialises in sexual abuse and self injury. Calls accepted from all over UK. Runs survivor group for women.)

BRITISH ASSOCIATION FOR COUNSELLING
1 Regent Place
Rugby TZ21 2PJ
Tel: 01788 578328
(Provides information on counsellors throughout UK-send s.a.e.)

BROADCASTING SUPPORT SERVICES
Westminster House
11 Portland Street
Manchester M1 3HU
Tel: 0161 455 1202
(Publishes 'Survivors Directory' giving details of national and local organisations offering help, and containing booklist for survivors and/or carers. Also offers off-air back-up/ helplines to radio and TV programmes on abuse for listeners or viewers seeking help and advice.)

CAMPAIGN FOR THE RIGHTS OF SURVIVORS OF SEXUAL ABUSE
c/o 29a Rye Hill Park
Peckham
London, SE15
Tel: 0181 452 6504
(A campaigning group which also offers information, advice and counselling.)

CHAR
(Housing Campaign for Single People)
Tel: 0171 833 2071
(Campaigns for young single homeless people and runs the '4 in 10 project' which supports agencies working with women homeless as a result of sexual abuse.)

CHILD ABUSE SURVIVOR NETWORK
PO Box 1
London N1 7SN
Tel: 0171 278 8414
(National organisation which helps adult survivors of serious abuse or maltreatment in childhood. Provides advice, information, newsletter, counselling pack, penfriends service – members only – and referral services for adult survivors. Send s.a.e. for information.)

CHILDLINE

2nd Floor, Royal Mail Buildings
50 Studd Street
London N1 OQW
Tel: 0171 239 1000 **administration**
0800 1111 **helpline**
0800 400222 **deaf/hearing–**
impaired helpline
0800 884444 **children in care**
helpline
Fax: 0171 239 1001
(Set up by Esther Rantzen and offers free 24 hour helpline, and counselling service for survivors of child abuse. Operates special phone lines for children in care, and for hearing impaired children. Whilst its principal focus is on children who need help, it also receives calls from adult survivors and perpetrators.)

CHILDLINE IN SCOTLAND

18 Albion Street
Glasgow
Scotland G1 1LH
Tel: 0800 1111 **helpline**

CROSS (Campaign for the Rights of Survivors of Abuse)

Tel: 0181 452 6504
(A national pressure group against child sexual abuse. Organises an annual march against abuse in London.)

DIRECTORY AND BOOK SERVICES

79 Copley Road
Doncaster DN1 2QP
Tel: 01302 768689 ·
(Publishes DABS National Resource Directory. Free information service and mail-order book service on sexual abuse. Provides a survivors pack, leaflets on self-help and lists of relevant local and national organisations.)

FIGHTING BACK

PO Box 1958,
London N8 7AW
(Issues quarterly newsletter by and for survivors-annual subscription £7.50, but sliding scale operates.)

ICAIR (Independent Care After Incest and Rape)

Tel: 01799 530520
01491 839925
01440 708174
(National network of helplines offering telephone, postal and face to face support. Specialises in recovery from childhood sexual abuse.Membership £10 including magazine.)

KIDSCAPE

152 Buckingham Palace Road
London SW1W 9TR
Tel: 0171 730 3300
(Disseminates information on sexual abuse and bullying, and on how parents can keep their children safe. Operates a bullying helpline.)

MOSAC (Mothers of Sexually Abused Children)
58 Kidbrook Grove
Blackheath
London SE3 OLJ
Tel: 0181 293 9990   helpline
(Provides a helpline for mothers/female carers of children who have been sexually abused, as well as a befriending service.)

NAPAC (National Association for People Abused in Childhood)
c/o NSPCC
42 Curtain Road
London EC2A 3NH
Tel: 0171 825 2803
Contact: Peter Saunders or Sylvia Tadd
(Currently being established as a national umbrella organisation for survivors of abuse to provide a 24–hour helpline, information exchange, and support.)

NSPCC (National Society for the Prevention of Cruelty to Children)
National Centre
42 Curtain Road
London EC2A 3NH
Tel: 0171 825 2500
        0171 825 2706/7 **Library**
        0800 800 500   **child protection helpline – 24–hr**
        0800 056 0566   **minicom helpline**
Fax: 0171 825 2525
(Acts to prevent the physical and mental abuse of children but provides counselling and referral services to survivors of any age. The Society's officers give advice, and where necessary take action to enforce the law for the protection of children. The helpline can give details of local survivors groups for adults.)

NATIONAL UNION OF STUDENTS
c/o Goldsmiths College S.U.
University of London
Lewisham Way
London SE14 6NW
Tel: 0181 692 1406
(Holds database of useful contacts for survivors.)

PAIN (Parents Against Injustice)
10 Waterlane
Bishops Stortford
Hertfordshire CM23 2JZ
Tel: 01279 656564
(Offers advice for people and families wrongly accused of abuse.)

PEPER HARROW FOUNDATION
14 Charterhouse Square
London EC1M 6AX
Tel: 0171 251 0672/6072
*(Runs residential therapeutic
communities for abused children and
adolescents.)*

RAPE CRISIS CENTRE
PO Box 69
London WC1X 9NJ
Tel: 0171 837 1600 **Counselling**
01923 241600 **Rape crisis and
sexual abuse line**
*(Provides telephone helpline and face-to-
face counselling for young and adult
women survivors.)*

REFUGE
PO Box 855
London W4 4JF
Tel: 0181 747 0133
0181 995 4430 **24 hour helpline**
*(Provides accommodation for women
and children fleeing domestic
violence/sexual abuse.)*

SAMARITANS
Central London Branch
46 Marshall Street
London W1
Tel: 0171 734 2800 **24 hour helpline**
0345 909090 **Linkline**
*(Has local branches. Offers 24 hour
helpline service for people feeling
suicidal or in despair.)*

SO SPEAK TRUST
Tel: 01702 619414
*(Publishes newsletter for workers,
survivors and allies.)*

SURVIVORS
PO Box 2470
London W2
Tel: 0171 833 3737
(helpline Tuesday and
Wednesday 7–10pm)
*(Provides help and support for men who
have been raped or sexually assaulted.)*

SURVIVORS COALITION
52–54 Featherstone Street
London EC1 8RT
*(A coalition of survivors and groups
campaigning for better resources,
legislation and information.)*

SURVIVORS ON THE NET
Tel: 01273 277943
*(Provides newsletter, magazine, and
24–hour internet support. Holds
national database of support groups.)*

VICTIMS SUPPORT
Cranmer House
39 Brixton Road
London SW9 6D2
Tel: 0171 735 9166
*(National organisation which will refer
to local support schemes.)*